New Amsterdam: The His

By Charles River Editors

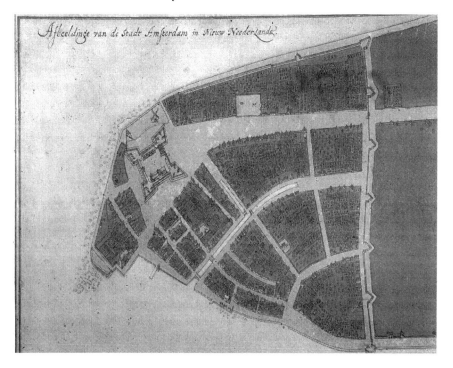

A colonial map of New Amsterdam

About Charles River Editors

Charles River Editors provides superior editing and original writing services across the digital publishing industry, with the expertise to create digital content for publishers across a vast range of subject matter. In addition to providing original digital content for third party publishers, we also republish civilization's greatest literary works, bringing them to new generations of readers via ebooks.

Sign up here to receive updates about free books as we publish them, and visit Our Kindle Author Page to browse today's free promotions and our most recently published Kindle titles.

Introduction

A 17th century illustration depicting New Amsterdam

New Amsterdam

Manhattan has long been part of a bustling community, even before it formed the backbone of New York City. Centuries before New York City became a shining city of steel that enthralled millions of immigrants, Lenni-Lenape Indians, an Algonquin-speaking tribe whose name means "the People," lived in what would become New York, New Jersey, and Pennsylvania. They had lived there for at least 1,500 years and were mainly hunters and gatherers who would use well-worn paths that would one day bear the names of Flatbush Avenue, King's Highway, and Broadway.

The first known European sightings of the island and its inhabitants were made by the Italian explorer Giovanni da Verrazzano in 1524 and by the black Portuguese explorer Estaban Gomez in 1526. After the Englishman Henry Hudson, under the aegis of the Dutch East India Company, sailed by Manhattan in 1609, he returned home with good news and bad news. Like the other explorers before him, he hadn't been able to find a water route to the Orient. He had, however, returned with maps (confiscated by the British) and beaver pelts. With that, it became clear that the region around the bay that would take Hudson's name was a very promising new territory for trade and settlement, which would become a serious bone of contention between the Dutch and the British for the rest of the century.

In 1614, another East India merchant, Adriaen Block, entered through the narrows of the East River between Queens and Randall's Island, a difficult and dangerous passage that later sank numerous ships and that Block named Hell's Gate (Hellegat). The European world would know the name "Manhates" when Block returned to the Netherlands with new and improved maps. After that further exploration, the Dutch returned to build settlements on the southern tip of Manhattan and elsewhere, and by 1626 trade was brisk both between the Native Americans and the European settlers and between the settlers and their mother countries.

1626 was also the year that the famous "purchase" of Manhattan took place, a transaction for which no record has survived. Peter Minuit, the Director-General of New Amsterdam, paid out sixty guilders' worth of trade goods like cloth, kettles, tools, and wampum—an amount that's come down in history as being worth $24. While that sounds perversely low today, accountant types like to speculate with this amount, if the Lenni-Lenapes had invested it at a 10% interest rate over the centuries, it would today be worth $117 quadrillion—enough to buy present-day Manhattan many, many times over.

Many such purchases took place, but because Native Americans and Europeans had very different concepts of what it meant to "own" or "sell" land, misunderstandings—and violence—would frequently break out on both sides. Minor (and often unsubstantiated) thefts of property could ignite the colonists' wrath, resulting in such bloody skirmishes as the Pig War (1640) and the Peach Tree War (1655), named for the items allegedly stolen.

When the West India Company, which presided over Dutch trade in the Americas, was created in 1621, the little settlement at the tip of Manhattan began to both grow and falter. When Willem Kieft arrived as director in 1638, it was already a sort of den of iniquity, full of "mischief and perversity," where residents were given over to smoking and drinking grog and beer. Under Kieft's reign, more land was acquired mostly through bloody, all-but-exterminating wars with the Native American population, whose numbers also dwindled at the hands of European-borne diseases.

New Amsterdam: The History of the Dutch Settlement Before It Became New York City chronicles the origins of the settlement and profiles the indigenous people who were there. Along with pictures of important people, places, and events, you will learn about New Amsterdam like never before, in no time at all.

New Amsterdam: The History of the Dutch Settlement Before It Became New York City

About Charles River Editors

Introduction

   Chapter 1: The Lenni-Lenape before the Arrival of the Dutch

   Chapter 2: The Netherlands as a World Power

   Chapter 3: The Lenni-Lenape and Dutch Settlers

   Chapter 4: The Early History of New Amsterdam

   Chapter 5: War

   Online Resources

   Bibliography

Chapter 1: The Lenni-Lenape before the Arrival of the Dutch

Before the Age of Discovery, the broad geographical region of present-day New York City north along the Hudson River to the Catskill Mountains, and the whole of New Jersey south to and around the Delaware Bay (including parts of present-day Delaware along with eastern Pennsylvania), was the homeland of the Lenni-Lenape people. The Lenni-Lenape were a village-dwelling people who spoke two closely-related dialects, Munsee and Unami, in the Algonquian language group. Munsee was spoken to the northward of the Delaware Water Gap and the Raritan River, and Unami was spoken to the southward of those geographical locations (see attached map). Lenni-Lenape in their language means "original people," and many other Algonquian-speaking tribes regarded them as their "grandfathers." Sometimes Lenni-Lenape have been referred to as the "Delaware Indians," but that is the name of an English Lord and is not their own name for themselves.

According to one of the Lenni-Lenape creation myths, as explained by a Lenni-Lenape elder in 1679 to a Dutch visitor to New York, the world started out as water everywhere. A tortoise was lying in the water, and when the tortoise raised its back, the water ran off, and this became the dry land. "The earth was now dry, and there grew a tree in the middle of the earth, and the root of this tree sent forth a sprout beside it, and there grew upon it a man, who was the first male. This man was then alone, and would have remained alone; but the tree bent over until its top touched the earth, and there shot therein another root, from which came forth another sprout, and there grew upon it the woman, and from these two are all men produced."

An 18th century portrait of a Lenni-Lenape chief

An early 19th century book called the *Walum Olum* purports to be the tale of how the Lenni-Lenape originated as a people somewhere to the west and then migrated to the region, where they lived after crossing a Big Water – perhaps the Mississippi River -- and having many other adventures, including conflicts with other Indian tribes along the way. It's an interesting tale, but ethnohistorians and archaeologists now generally regard the book as fake.

The Lenni-Lenape population, which numbered around 10,000 people when the first whites arrived, was divided into a multitude of smaller individually-named bands, each having several hundred or more members. Each band had its own territory generally corresponding to a watershed or section of river. Some of these bands might unite in the face of a common enemy.

However, there was no overarching political structure for the Lenni-Lenape as a whole. Most of the time, the bands operated autonomously. Each band had its own chief called a "sachem", but his authority was limited to his ability to persuade the band members; for important decisions, all of the adult male members of the band met in a general council. Sachems were expected to redistribute goods to maintain the approval of their followers, and they organized group hunts and were responsible for making sure that band justice was done.

Bands interacted through the cooperative extraction of resources, such as gathering at the same fishing spots, attending occasional festivals, and through intermarriage. Kinship was the most important social organizing principle, and descent was matrilineal. Thus a man might have his closest relationships with his sister's children rather than those by his wife. Serious crimes were rare among the Lenni-Lenape. A murder could be avenged by the next of kin, or recompense could be made from the murderer or their kin group. In general, they were extremely civil to relatives, friends, and visitors alike and practiced the sharing of food stuffs and other necessities, more so than many Christians, as was remarked by them later.

For sustenance, the Lenni-Lenape grew the famous "Three Sisters" – maize, beans and squash – and tobacco was also grown. Men using stone axes helped with clearing new fields, but tending to the fields was women's work (using a digging stick and hoes). Corn was dried and stored in mat-lined pits, to be pounded later by women into corn meal in a mortar made out of a hollowed-out log, while nuts and berries were gathered in season. The men hunted deer, bear and other animals with bows and arrows, caught them with snares or drove them with fires to where they could be killed. Fires were also set to the woods on a regular basis to make the hunting easier by removing the underbrush. Cornmeal mixed with water was baked into a bread under the ashes of a fire or was boiled into "sappaan," a mush sometimes flavored with maple syrup. A beaver tail fried in bear fat was considered a particular delicacy. Birds like the passenger pigeon, turkey, and ducks were hunted as well. Fish were taken with nets or lines or were trapped in weirs. The fish and animals were cooked whole with the entrails usually not removed. Dogs were sometimes eaten when they ran out of other food. Water was the only beverage. Shellfish were collected for eating or were smoked for later use.

Out of the shells of the quahog clam and the whelk found along this stretch of the northeastern Atlantic coast, small dark blue and white beads were manufactured. This *wampum* (called "sewan" by the Dutch) was strung together in lengths or was woven into belts to be used for decorative and ceremonial purposes. Wampum was also used as compensation for crimes.

The Lenni-Lenape males in the warmer times of the year wore only a soft deerskin breechclout about a yard and a half long to cover their private parts, tied with a snakeskin around the waist and hanging down with a flap in the front. Women wore a skirt. When the weather became colder, a mantle made out of bear or raccoon or beaver or wildcat or some other animal was worn with the fur side turned inward. Men also put on leggings. Cloaks were made out of turkey feathers, cleverly tied together with hemp strings. Moccasins were made out of deer or moose skins and socks made from corn husks.

Along with *wampum* strings, copper rings, long tufts of red-dyed deer's hair, and porcupine quills were used for clothing decoration. Men's hair was worn long or it was shaved into a scalplock greased to stand up straight with bear grease. On the head, a feathered headdress might be worn, but with the feathers standing straight up (unlike the feathered headdresses of the Plains Indians). Facial hair was deemed to be highly unattractive on men and was removed using a mollusk shell as tweezers. Women bound their long hair into a covered knot behind them. The face and body might be painted and tattooed with pictures of beasts and birds, and stinky animal grease was liberally applied during the summer as protection against insects and sunburn. A pouch made from the skin of a small animal was worn to hold valuables. Along with a bow and arrows, a wooden or hide shield and a club were carried by men as their technology for war.

The prominent Quaker and founder of Pennsylvania, William Penn, who had many peaceful dealings with the Lenni-Lenape, described the different physical appearance of the Indians: "For their persons, they are generally tall, streight [sic], well-built and of singular Proportion; they tread strong and clever, and mostly walk with a lofty Chin: of Complexion, Black, but by design, as the Gypsies in England: They grease themselves with Bears-fat clarified, and using no defense against Sun or Weather, their skins must needs be swarthy; Their Eye is little and black, not unlike a straight-look't Jew. The thick Lip and flat Nose, so frequent with the East-Indians and Blacks, are not common to them; for I have seen as comely European-like faces among them of both, as on your side the Sea; and truly an Italian Complexion hath not much more of the White, and the Noses of several of them have as much as the Roman."

A depiction of William Penn dealing with Lenni-Lenape natives in Pennsylvania

The Lenni-Lenape lived in round or square wigwams or in longhouses built out of a frame of bent-over tree branches or saplings covered with chestnut bark, reed mats and hides. The longhouses were up to 60 feet long and 15 feet wide, with low doors that required stooping to enter at each end. They were shared by a number of related families but with a separate fire and cook pot for each family from which people ate whenever they felt hungry. An opening in the roof of the wigwam or longhouse let the fire's smoke out. To sleep, people lay on mats on the ground with their feet pointed toward the fire. There was no furniture to sit on; people either sat on the ground or squatted on their ankles. Some of the dwellings had carved faces or images inside them, although these were found mainly in the dwellings of the chiefs. Household ware consisted of a calabash to hold water, bowls and spoons made out of a calabash, small baskets for corn and beans, and knives. Wild hemp was used to make rope as well as baskets, bags, and purses interwoven with porcupine quills.

Lenni-Lenape villages were sometimes surrounded by a stockade. People moved from location to location within their territory on a seasonal basis according to where the best food sources were to be found. In the winter, most people dispersed to hunting camps located in the back country. Corn fields were relocated to new land when the fertility of the soil was depleted, although the Indians might return to the same old field again after the passage of some years.

Marriage among the Lenni-Lenape was not accompanied by any particular ceremony except for the prospective groom presenting the woman with a gift or offering that she accepted to indicate her willingness. Girls married at the age of 13 or 14, and boys did at 17 or 18 after they had proven their abilities in the hunt. Polygamy was present although not commonplace, with some males, especially the chiefs, taking two or three wives. Divorce was equally easy to accomplish, with the children who belonged to her matrilineage going with the mother.

Women stayed in a menstrual hut during their menses and were subject to taboos pertaining to what they could eat. During the final stages of pregnancy, a woman went to an isolated shelter where she brought forth her baby without any assistance. She then immersed herself and her newborn in a cold brook before returning without much fuss to her domestic duties. The baby was strapped to a cradleboard and carried on the mother's back. The Lenni-Lenape had a great affection for their children and rarely applied any form of physical punishment. During the two years that the child was breastfeeding, no sexual intercourse was performed.

The ability to swim was commonplace. Two kinds of boats were built: Dugouts from logs that were laborious burned and scraped a little bit at a time and canoes covered with bark sewn together with sinews. Large dugouts could hold as many as twelve to fourteen people. Otherwise, transportation was by foot. A network of trails connected villages to each other and to locations for fishing and hunting. In the deep snows of winter, snow shoes were used.

The Lenni-Lenape believed in the existence of a Supreme Being, "Kicheron," but Kicheron was a hands-off kind of deity. More important to them were the spiritual powers ("manitou") that inhabited all the animate and inanimate things, and dreams and visions were very important among the Lenni-Lenape. Children were not named until their parents had a vision about an appropriate name. Young males sought a vision of a totemic animal who would continue to assist them throughout life.

A rigorous round of fasting and vision-questing accompanied preparations for going on the hunt. A successful hunt was followed by a celebratory dance, and animal fat was thrown into the fire to thank the *manitou* for the success. A community celebration was held after corn harvest in the autumn which morphed into the "Big House Ceremony" of reservation years. The medicine man was a "Me-ta-ow." The sweatlodge was used to cleanse the body and to treat ailments, but it was also used for spiritual purification.

The dead among the Lenni-Lenape were buried in a sitting position covered with tree boughs and then earth. Some of the dead person's belongings and some *wampum* would be placed in the grave for use in the other world, but the rest of their belongings would be redistributed. Relatives in mourning might paint their faces black for a year, whereas red face paint was used to signify that something joyful had happened, and the dead person's name was not mentioned or ever used again. The grave would be carefully tended and enclosed with a fence, and an evergreen tree might be planted next to it. The Lenni-Lenape believed that a person's soul continued its existence after death, going to some happy place to the southward. There was no belief in sin and the dreadful consequences of eternal damnation, as among Christians.

As a result, this was how the Lenni-Lenape lived up until the early 17th century, when things changed with the arrival of hairy-faced white men in boats larger than the Lenni-Lenape had ever seen before and propelled by what looked like billowing clouds.

Chapter 2: The Netherlands as a World Power

During the 17th century, the Netherlands, despite having only 1.5 million people in 1600, became a global maritime and trading power. By contrast, France at that same time had 20 million people, Spain had 8 million, and England had 5 million. Nevertheless, Amsterdam became one of the most important urban centers in the world and the location of the world's first stock market, and Dutch merchant ships and pirates plied the Atlantic, the Indian Ocean and the Pacific. The Dutch acquired colonies in the East Indies, where they seized control of the spice trade from the Portuguese, and in the West Indies, they acquired a number of islands from the Spanish (several of which are still Dutch today). They became the only Westerners who were allowed to trade with Shogunate Japan from a small island next to Nagasaki. All of this imperialism generated enormous amounts of wealth that flowed into the Netherlands.

Netherlands means "Low Country." Located largely on the deltas of the Rhine and Maas Rivers, much of it consisted of sand dunes and peat bogs until, centuries ago, humans began building dikes, pumping out water and laboriously reclaiming the land. Much of the land falls below sea level. As an old saying goes, "God created the earth, but the Dutch created the Netherlands." The long struggle with nature is an important part of the Dutch identity.

The Dutch identity as a political entity was achieved through the process of fighting a long and brutal war of resistance against rule by the Spanish Hapsburgs starting in 1568. In 1581, the seven northern provinces – Holland, Zeeland, Utrecht, Gelderland, Overijssel, Friesland, and Groningen – declared their independence, and back and forth warfare took place on land and the sea, with the Dutch receiving some much-needed assistance from England's Queen Elizabeth. Thousands of civilians were massacred by the rampaging Spanish armies, and on the water, Dutch "sea beggars" attacked and harassed the Spanish fleet while pro-Spanish privateers operating out of Dunkirk did the same against Dutch shipping.

The attempt in 1588 by the Spanish Armada to subjugate the Netherlands and England by invading England was defeated, and in 1609, with both sides totally exhausted, fighting was suspended during a 12-year truce made between the new Spanish king and the now United Provinces. However, when the truce expired in 1621, fighting resumed once more, and it was not until 1648 and the Peace of Westphalia that ended the 30 Years War (or 80 Years War in the case of the Dutch) that the independence of the Netherlands was solidified for good, with the remaining 10 southern provinces – the constituents of the modern state of Belgium – continuing under Spanish Hapsburg control.

Although there were other issues behind the revolt, like heavy taxation, the war was in large part a religious revolt. Many of the Dutch, especially in the northern and western provinces, had become Protestants, followers primarily of the French theologian John Calvin (although there were some Lutherans and Anabaptists present as well). Calvinism as institutionalized in the Dutch Reformed Church would become the officially-recognized faith of independent Netherlands, but Philip II, the ultra-pious king of Spain, was determined to restore Catholicism through the strict use of the Inquisition against "heretics," and the Catholics were strongest in the 10 southern provinces. Religious differences between north and south were accentuated because of the migration of Protestants and Catholics across the border during the long war.

Philip II of Spain

Within the Netherlands itself, the Calvinists struggled with each other over doctrinal issues. With no denomination or sect able to impose itself on the whole of society, the Netherlands during the 17th century became a place of refuge for free-thinkers and members of heterodox religious groups. As exemplified by the philosopher Baruch Spinoza, the Netherlands was one of the few places in Europe where Jews could live and work without being persecuted. Science and inquiry flourished in the tolerant atmosphere where books could be published without censorship. The microscope was invented by the Dutch instrument-maker Antonie van Leeuwenhoek, and unlike Galileo in Italy, he did not have to worry about being dragged before a tribunal for what he saw through his lenses that might challenge what was stated in the Scriptures. This was also the age of the great painters like Rembrandt, Vermeer, and Franz Hals, who painted portraits of the proudly assured members of the Dutch bourgeoisie.

Politically, most actual governing in the Dutch Republic remained decentralized at the level of the seven different provinces, but the States General, a parliament in which the provinces were equally represented, took on more and more executive powers. Meanwhile, the main military leaders of the Netherlands came from the House of Orange. Prince William I organized and led the revolt against Spain until his assassination in 1584, and his son, Maurice, then became the *stadtholder* (steward) of the United Provinces and the principle leader of the resistance. Maurice was succeeded in that role after he died in 1625 by his brother, Frederick Henry.

William I of Orange

Much of the Dutch success against Spanish professional forces that were often numerically superior was due to their recruitment and training of a professional army. Prince Maurice of Orange was the innovator of new methods for maximizing the use of firepower by having his soldiers lined up in ranks and drilled to fire their volleys in turn, and the Dutch methodology spread throughout Europe. Much of the revolt and war, however, involved not pitched battles in the field but long protracted sieges of heavily-fortified cities and towns.

The other part of the Dutch success in war had to do with their capabilities at sea, where the Dutch emerged supreme over the Spanish on the way to developing the most powerful navy in the world. In October 1639, the Dutch destroyed much of the Spanish fleet at the Battle of the Downs off the coast of England, a blow from which Spain never recovered as a mighty naval power.

Starting out with the voyages of Columbus westward in 1492 and Vasco de Gama going east around the bottom of Africa in 1498, Spain and Portugal established territorial colonies in the Americas and trading posts in East Asia. To try to catch up with their enemies (Portugal was also ruled by the same King as Spain from 1580-1640) in the lucrative trading enterprises and to hurt them in other parts of the world, the Dutch first attempted to find a shorter route to the riches of the Orient by going north around Russia. Three expeditions backed by Amsterdam merchants that went looking for such a Northeast Passage in the 1590s, led by William Barents were failures, with Barents dying in the High Arctic in 1597.

Barents

More successfully, another Dutch sea captain, Cornelius de Houtman, after spending time in Lisbon studying how the Portuguese did things, led an expedition of four Dutch ships to what is now Indonesia in 1595-97. Although the natives were treated with brutality, this opened up a highly profitable direct Dutch trade in nutmeg, cloves, and other spices. The Dutch would then gradually wrest away control of that spice trade from the Portuguese and exercise a monopoly over it.

Another existing Portuguese trade was the slave trade. During the 1590s, Dutch ships started trading on the Gold Coast of Africa (present-day Ghana), from which they obtained slaves and began to sell them in the Americas. The first slaves that came to what would become the United States arrived in Virginia in 1619 aboard a Dutch ship, while in 1600, a Dutch ship reached Japan. The next year, the Dutch were found in Canton, and in 1610 the first cargo of Asian tea arrived in Amsterdam. A permanent Dutch base near the spices was established in 1619 at Batavia (today's Djakarta in Indonesia), so the Dutch more than made up for a late start with their naval superiority and business acumen.

Dutch success in ventures launched both east and west was aided greatly by the formation of two joint-stock companies: the East India Company (known by its Dutch initials, VOC) and the West India Company. The VOC was founded in 1602 and the WIC in 1621, and both companies were granted full trading monopolies by the Dutch government in the respective geographical zones assigned to them and acted there as *de facto* governing bodies, although under the supervision of the States General. The WIC's most profitable coup came when an admiral in their employ captured the entire Spanish silver fleet *en route* from Mexico to Seville in 1628. However, the principal source of the company's profits came from slavery, through the sugar plantations it operated in the Caribbean and South America and as the world's largest trans-Atlantic purveyor of slaves to the other colonial powers. As a result, both the VOC and the WIC would play roles in the history of New Amsterdam.

Stimulated by the needs of this global trade and of the long war with Spain and Portugal, ship-building was a major Dutch industry. At its peak, the Dutch had more ships on the seas than Spain, France, England and all of the other European nations combined, peaking at 6,000 ships with 48,000 sailors. One reason for this rapid Dutch success on the seas was their invention of the *fluyt* (flyboat). The *fluyt* was a round-bellied, shallow-drafted ship designed to carry the maximum amount of cargo cheaply from port to port. It was cheap to build and needed fewer sailors to handle it. With the *fluyt*, the Dutch came to dominate trade in grain with the Baltic, making Amsterdam into the most important grain market in Europe. Dutch ships also brought back timber and naval stores like masts, pitch and tar directly from the Baltics lowering their costs of ship-building.

The Dutch were likewise a major presence in fishing, with 1500 boats catching herring on the Dogger Banks off the England coast and harpooning whales in far northern Spitzenberg. Whale blubber was rendered into oil for lamps and for making soap, and the herring fed Catholics on the numerous meatless saints' days in Europe.

Dutch farming was the first in the world to go through an agricultural revolution. Systems of crop rotation were developed to maintain the soil's fertility, and animal manure and town waste were carefully utilized because the land base was so limited. Intensive market gardening, along with imported wheat, fed the growing cities and towns. The Dutch Holstein breed produced milk for butter and cheese for which the towns of Gouda and Edam became famous. Other cash crops grown in the commercialized Dutch agriculture were flax (for linen), hemp (for ropes), rape plant (for oil seeds), hops (for beer), tobacco, and dye plants to be used in the technologically state-of-the-art textile industry. Countless windmills worked to grind grain and pump out water to keep the *polders* dry.

Thus, the small, densely-settled, urbanized country of the Netherlands became, in the words of the historian Jan de Vries, the first modern capitalist economy. Amsterdam's harbor bustled with ships flying the flags of many nations, its warehouses bulged with goods from all parts of the world, and it housed commodity exchanges and Bank of Amsterdam. Refugees came to the Dutch capital from the former trading center of Antwerp (captured by the Spanish in 1585 and then atrophied due to closure of its sea access by a Dutch blockade) and other places in the southern provinces, and they brought with them their capital and skills. With men and women migrating from Germany, Scandinavia and other places to find good-paying work, Amsterdam swelled from a population of 30,000 during the early years of the revolt to almost 105,000 in 1622 and to over 200,000 in the 1660s. As a contemporary said, Amsterdam was "the warehouse of the World, the Seat of Opulence, the rendezvous of riches and the darling of the gods."

Understandably proud of their international center, when the Dutch established a settlement in North America, it's no surprise they would name it "New Amsterdam."

Chapter 3: The Lenni-Lenape and Dutch Settlers

According to one native informant for the Dutch, the first Europeans the Lenni-Lenape encountered were either Spanish or Portuguese, which is possible since one or more Portuguese sea captains made voyages along the east coast of what is now the United States in the early 1500s. The first encounter that was documented from the European side involved the Florentine sea captain, Giovanni de Verrazzano, who explored the east coast starting in what is now North Carolina and working his way north to Nova Scotia in 1524 while employed by the French King Francis I, who wanted his own cut of the New World. In New York harbor, Verrazzano reports that they found "the country on its banks well-peopled, the Inhabitants not differing much from the others, being dressed out with the feathers of birds of various colors. They came towards us with evident delight, raising loud shouts of admiration, and showing us where we could most securely land with our boat." 30 or more canoes filled Indians came out to see the strangers, but the visit between the two cultures was truncated when bad weather forced Verrazzano to leave and continue his voyage northward.

Giovanni de Verrazzano

It is likely that the ships of other European nations --fishermen, traders and the like – made trips to the same region during the 16th century, but it was not until the 1609 voyage of the Englishman Henry Hudson, employed by Dutch merchants from the East India Company, that there were other written records of the area, including records of encounters with the native inhabitants, the Lenni-Lenape. Hudson sailed in his *fluyt*, the *Half Moon*, with a crew of 18 or 20 men, partly Dutch and partly English, and they tried to find a Northeast Passage to the riches of China by going over the top of the world. However, he found his way blocked by sea ice and had to deal with cold and mutinous sailors. Giving up – he had made two previously unsuccessful searches for a Northeast Passage on behalf of the London-based Muscovy Company – Hudson turned his ship around and sailed westward and south to look for a Northwest Passage instead. His friend, Captain John Smith, one of the leaders of the new English colony at Jamestown, Virginia, had suggested that he might find something around latitude 40 degrees.

A replica of Hudson's ship donated by the Dutch to the United States

After surveying the coastline as far south as North Carolina and finding nothing, Hudson headed back north up the coast, where he arrived outside New York harbor on September 3. Hudson's and his men's interactions with the natives they encountered were mixed. When the *Half Moon* arrived near New York harbor, probably anchoring off Sandy Hook or Staten Island, Lenni-Lenape came out to their ship in canoes to trade with them, indicating in their behavior that this was something which they had done before: "This day the people of the countrey came aboord of us, seeming very glad of our comming, and brought greene tobacco, and gave us of it for knives and beads. They goe in deere skins loose, well dressed. They have yellow copper. They desire cloathes, and are very civill. They have great store of maize or Indian wheate, whereof they make good bread. The countrey is full of great and tall oakes."

The next day, Hudson's mate, Robert Juet, recorded again in his logbook, "Our men went on land there, and saw great store of men, women, and children, who gave them tabacco at their comming on land. So they went up into the woods, and saw great store of very goodly oakes and some currants. For one of them came brought some dryed, and gave me some, which were sweet and good. This day many of the people came aboard, some in mantles of feathers, and some in skinnes of divers sorts of good furres. Some women also came to us with hempe. They had red copper tabacco pipes, and other things of copper, they did weare about their neckes. At night they went on land againe, so wee rode very quiet, but durst not trust them."

On the day after that, however, a boat sent out to explore and take soundings of the water depth had a violent scrape with some Lenni-Lenape warriors in two large boats, one carrying 12 men and the other with 14. One English crewman was slain with an arrow through his throat and two other men were wounded in the fight. The Europeans found themselves at a disadvantage because it started raining and the matches for their arquebuses (guns) wouldn't light. Then the men became lost in the darkness and paddled around the whole night. From Juet's account, it is not clear how this one encounter with the Indians became violent, but when more Lenni-Lenape came aboard the *Half Moon* two days later to trade tobacco and "Indian wheat" for knives and beads, they showed no signs that they knew of the violent encounter.

Regardless, the sailors of the *Half Moon* were now on their guard. On the next morning, "Two great canoes came aboord full of men; the one with their bowes and arrowes, and the other in shew of buying of knives to betray us; but we perceived their intent. Wee tooke two of them to have kept them, and put red coates on them, and would not suffer the other to come neere us. So they went on land, and two other came aboord in a canoe; we tooke the one and let the other goe; but hee which wee had taken, got up and leapt over-boord. Then we weighed and went off into the channell of the river, and anchored there all night."

The following day, the *Half Moon* went a distance up the river, where "the people of the country came aboord of us, making shew of love, and gave us tabacco and Indian wheat, and departed for that night; but we durst not trust them."

A similar event took place on September 12th: "This morning, at our first rode in the river, there came eight and twentie canoes full of men, women and children to betray us: but we saw their intent, and suffered none of them to come aboord of us. At twelve of the clocke they departed. They brought with them oysters and beanes, whereof wee bought some. They have great tabacco pipes of yellow copper, and pots of earth to dresse their meate in."

On September 12, 1609, Hudson started an ascent of the river that is named after him today (although the Dutch actually named it not for him but for their *stadholder*, Prince Maurice of Orange). On the 13th, somewhere farther upriver on the upper part of Manhattan Island – the later-to-be-famous name is used in Juet's account and means "the place where wood is procured for bows and arrows" in the Munsee language – another friendly encounter with Indians took place, although the sailors remained wary and took measures to prevent possible trouble. "At seven of the clocke in the morning, as the floud came we weighed, and turned foure miles into the river. The tide being done wee anchored. Then there came foure canoes aboord: but we suffered none of them to come into our ship. They brought great store of very good oysters aboord, which we bought for trifles."

By the 14th of September, the *Half Moon* had sailed beyond West Point and was entering the region of the Catskill Mountains, which took them beyond the territory of the Lenni-Lenape. The two captive Lenni-Lenape natives escaped ship, jumping out of a port and swimming to shore. Farther north was the territory of another Algonquian-speaking people, the Mahicans. Here, Juet reported that "wee found very loving people, and very old men: where wee were well used." These Indians came aboard the *Half Moon* from their canoes on the east bank near present-day Hudson, New York and "brought us eares of Indian corne, and pompions, and tabacco : which wee bought for trifles." Except for the saltwater oysters, this was the same trading stock as had been brought them by the Lenni-Lenape.

What interested Hudson and his men much more is that these Indians also brought something else. On the 18th, Indians showed up with more fruits of the land which they again bought for trifles, but the Indians brought "bevers skinnes and otters skinnes, which we bought for beades, knives, and hatchets." To test these Indians to see if they "had any treacherie in them," Hudson and his mate took some of them below to his cabin where they plied them with wine and *aqua vitae* (distilled spirits). Everyone was reported to be very merry, although they were not used to the alcohol and did not know how to handle it. An old chief became drunk and passed out, sleeping the night quietly on the ship with some strings of wampum that his friends had brought to make him feel better. The other Indians came back at noon and were glad to find that all was well. "So at three of the clocke in the afternoone they came aboord, and brought tabacco, and more beades, and gave them to our master, and made an oration, and shewed him all the countrey round about. Then they sent one of their companie on land, who presently returned, and brought a great platter full of venison dressed by themselves; and they caused him to eate with them: then they made him reverence and departed, all save the old man that lay aboord. This night, at ten of the clocke, our boat returned in a showre of raine from sounding of the river; and found it to bee at an end for shipping to goe in. For they had beene up eight or nine leagues, and found but seven foot water, and unconstant soundings."

Returning back down the river, the *Half Moon* was approached again by some Mahicans. "The sixe and twentieth was faire weather, and the wind at south a stifle gale; wee rode still. In the morning our carpenter went on land, with our masters mate and foure more of our companie, to cut wood. This morning, two canoes came up the river from the place where we first found loving people, and in one of them was the old man that had lyen aboord of us at the other place. He brought another old man with him, which brought more stropes of bead.es and gave them to our master, and shewed him all the countrey there about as though it were at his command. So he made the two old men dine with him, and the old mans wife: for they brought two old women, and two young maidens of the age of sixteene or seventeene yeares with them, who behaved themselves very modestly. Our master gave one of the old men a knife, and they gave him and us tabacco. And at one of the clocke they departed downe the river, making signes that wee should come downe to them; for wee were within two leagues of the place where they dwelt."

To the great sorrow of the Indians, when the *Half Moon* reached their location the next day; since the wind was blowing in a favorable direction for a change, Hudson decided to take advantage of it and continue on downriver. When they reached the mountains again on the 29th, more Indians approached them in canoes and came aboard with "Indian wheat," which they bought for "trifles." The word seemed to have spread regarding what the whites were most interested in because the next day, the "people of the country" came with small skins to trade which they bought for knives along with "trifles." Juet noted that where they were moored was "a very pleasant place to build a Towne on," and later the Dutch settlers would found Poughkeepsie nearby.

Hudson and his men, who were interested in potential minerals to exploit, too, were also intrigued when some Indians brought a stone aboard "like to an emery (a stone used by glasiers to cut glasse), it would cut iron or Steele: yet being bruised small, and water put to it, it made a colour like blacke lead glistering: it is also good for painters colours." Then, on October 1st, the "people of the montaynes came aboord us, wondring at our ship and weapons. We bought some small skinnes of them for trifles."

Nevertheless, the encounters Hudson and his sailors had with the indigenous people living in that vicinity, whether Mahicans or perhaps Lenni-Lenape, ended on an exceedingly sour and violent note:

> "This afternoone, one canoe kept hanging under our sterne with one man in it, which we could not keepe from thence, who got up by our rudder to the cabin

window, and stole out my pillow, and two shirts, and two bandeleeres. Our masters mate shot at him, and strooke him on the brest, and killed him. Whereupon all the rest fled away, some in their canoes, and so leapt out of them into the water. We manned our boat, and got our things againe. Then one of them that swamme got hold of our boat, thinking to overthrow it. But our cooke tooke a sword, and cut off one of his hands, and he was drowned. By this time the ebbe was come, and we weighed and got downe two leagues: by that time it was darke. So we anchored in foure fathomes water, and rode well.

"The second, faire weather. At break of day wee weighed, the wind being at north-west, and got downe seven leagues; then the floud was come strong, so we anchored. Then came one of the savages that swamme away from us at our going up the river with many other, thinking to betray us. But wee perceived their intent, and suffered none of them to enter our ship. Whereupon two canoes full of men, with their bowes and arrowes shot at us after our sterne: in recompence whereof we discharged sixe muskets, and killed two or three of them. Then above an hundred of them came to a point of land to shoot at us. There I shot a falcon at them, and killed two of them: whereupon the rest fled into the woods. Yet they manned off another canoe with nine or ten men, which came to meet us. So I shot at it also a falcon, and shot it through, and killed one of them. Then our men with their muskets killed three or foure more of them.1 So they went their way; within a while after wee got downe two leagues beyond that place, and anchored in a bay, cleere from all danger of them on the other side of the river, where we saw a very good piece of ground: and hard by it there was a cliffe, that looked of the colour of a white greene, as though it were either copper or silver myne: and I thinke it to be one of them, by the trees that grow upon it. For they be all burned, and the other places are greene as grasse; it is on that side of the river that is called Manna-hata. There we saw no people to trouble us: and rode quietly all night; but had much wind and raine."

After more wind and rain, fair weather came back on October 4th, and the *Half Moon* went out to sea and set sail for its return voyage to England to carry back all the interesting news, which would spread quickly and stimulate interest in sending more ships to the same area. After landing in England, Hudson was arrested for working for the Dutch enemies of the English Crown. The next year, Hudson resumed his futile search for a Northwest Passage, dying on a voyage that took him to what would be named Hudson's Bay after a mutinous crew set him adrift.

Meanwhile, the Lenni-Lenape had their own strong oral traditions of their encounter with Hudson and the *Half Moon* on Manhattan Island These were collected by the Moravian missionary John Heckewelder, who spent a great deal of time with the Indians in the second half of the 18th century. According to Heckewelder's informants, the Indians who first spied Hudson's ship in the distance were stunned by what their eyes saw. Some concluded that the ship was an uncommonly large fish or some other animal, while others thought it was a very large house. "It was at length agreed among those who were spectators, that as this phenomenon moved towards the land, whether or not it was an animal, or anything that had life in it, it would be well to inform all the Indians on the inhabited islands of what they had seen, and put them on their guard. Accordingly, they sent runners and watermen off to carry the news to their scattered chiefs, that these might send off in every direction for the warriors to come in. These arriving in numbers, and themselves viewing the strange appearance, and that it was actually moving towards them (the entrance of the river or bay), concluded it to be a large canoe or house, in which the Mannitto (great or supreme being) himself was, and that he probably was coming to visit them. By this time the chiefs of the different tribes were assembled on York Island, and were deliberating on the manner in which they should receive their Mannitto on his arrival. Every step had been taken to be well provided with plenty of meat for a sacrifice; the women were required to prepare the best of victuals; idols or images were examined and put in order; and a grand dance was supposed not only to be an agreeable entertainment for the Mannitto, but might, with the addition of a sacrifice, contribute towards appeasing him, in case he was angry with them. The conjurors were also set to work, to determine what the meaning of this phenomenon was, and what the result would be. Both to these, and to the chiefs and wise men of the nation, men, women, and children were looking up for advice and protection. Between hope and fear, and in confusion, a dance commenced. While in this situation, fresh runners arrive, declaring it a house of various colours, and crowded with living creatures. It now appears to be certain that it is the great Mannitto bringing them some kind of game, such as they had not before; but other runners soon after arriving, declare it a large house of various colours, full of people, yet of quite a different colour than they (the Indians) are of; that they were also dressed in a different manner from them, and that one in particular appeared altogether red, which must be the Mannitto himself. They are soon hailed from the vessel, though in a language they do not understand; yet they shout (or yell) in their way. Many are for running off to the woods, but are pressed by others to stay, in order not to give offence to their visitors, who could find them out, and might destroy them."

A "canoe" (ship's boat) brought a party of white men ashore from the ship. The red-suited "Manitou" (Henry Hudson) stepped off and, accompanied by two of his men while the rest guarded the boat, approached and saluted the Indians whose chiefs and councilors had gathered in a large circle. The Indians return a friendly salute, but they were bewildered. "They are lost in admiration, both as to the colour of the skin (of these whites) as also to their manner of dress, yet most as to the habit of him who wore the red clothes, which shone with something they could not account for. He must be the great Mannitto (supreme being) they think, but why should he have a white skin? A large hockhack [Indian name for a container carrying liquid] is brought forward by one of the (supposed) Mannitto's servants, and from this a substance is poured out into a small cup (or glass) and handed to the Mannitto. The (expected) Mannitto drinks; has the glass filled again, and hands it to the chief next to him to drink. The chief receives the glass, but only smelleth at it, and passes it on to the next chief, who does the same. The glass thus passes through the circle without the contents being tasted by any one; and is upon the point of being returned again to the red-clothed man, when one of their number, a spirited man and great warrior, jumps up, harangues the assembly on the impropriety of returning the glass with the contents in it; that the same was handed them by the Mannitto in order that they should drink it, as he himself had done before them; that this would please him; but to return what he had given to them might provoke him, and be the cause of their being destroyed by him. And that since he believed it for the good of the nation that the contents offered them should be drank, and as no one was willing to drink it he would, let the consequence be what it would; and that it was better for one man to die, than a whole nation to be destroyed. He then took the glass and bidding the assembly a farewell, drank it off. Every eye was fixed on their resolute companion to see what an effect this would have upon him, and he soon beginning to stagger about, and at last dropping to the ground, they bemoan him. He falls into a sleep, and they view him as expiring. He awakes again, jumps up, and declares that he never felt himself before so happy as after he had drank the cup. Wishes for more. His wish is granted; and the whole assembly soon join him, and become intoxicated."

After the intoxication was over – during which the white men remained for safety on their ship -- the man dressed in red returned and distributed presents, including beads, axes, hoes, stockings and others articles. The Indians understood through the use of signs that he promised that they would come again next year, bring more presents and stay with them for a while, in which case they would need some land on which they could plant crops to feed themselves.

According to the same oral traditions of the Indians taken down by Heckewelder, the ship did in fact return the following year, as promised. However, that could not have been Henry Hudson's *Half Moon*, since they were in the High Arctic searching for a Northwest Passage. Possibly, this was another Dutch ship captained by Hendrick Christiaensen, who came to the area of Hudson's discovery in 1610 or 1611, but little else is known about the voyage from the European records. According to the Lenni-Lenape's oral traditions, people on this second ship did remain and obtained land from them, but while there were several other voyages that came and went, no Dutch stayed in the area of New York City until 1614, when a fur trading post, Ft. Nassau, was built near the river's head of navigation at today's Albany in the Mahican territory. From that point forward, the *Swannakens* (the Indian term for the Dutch, meaning "salt water people") and many of the Indians enjoyed regular relationships.

Chapter 4: The Early History of New Amsterdam

The news of Henry Hudson's discoveries, once they became known, aroused great interest in the Netherlands, but for whatever reason, the East India Company (VOC), which had sponsored his trip, did not follow up, probably because it was outside of its assigned geographical region. That task was taken up by other Amsterdam merchants, the bulk of whom were Lutheran refugees from the Catholic southern provinces that were still controlled by Spain. Several competing sets of merchants sent ships to the region starting in 1612, and they demonstrated the benefits of future ventures by returning with furs. This free-for-all was great for the Indians because the competition drove up the fur prices, but it was not so good for the different merchants who were unable to come to a fair agreement among themselves. Thus, in 1615, the States General chartered the New Netherland Company, giving it a monopoly on the trade for three years.

Beaver furs, in particular, were in high demand in Europe. Soft pliable felt for gentlemen's hats was made from the inner hairs of the beaver pelt, but beavers in most parts of Europe had already been hunted out. On the other hand, beavers were abundant in North America, and the French in New France (Canada), the Dutch, and, to a lesser extent, the English in the New England colonies all employed Indians to trap beavers for them. In return, the Indians eagerly acquired all kinds of trade goods, from the utilitarian to the decorative.

Some did not understand what the goods were for at first; Heckewelder relayed a humorous anecdote about some Lenni-Lenape who were given metal axes and wore the heavy objects around their necks as ornaments until whites showed them what they were supposed to be used for. Regardless, it didn't take long for many natives to become dependent on trading furs for these articles, giving up traditional practices such as chipping flints for edged-tools and projectile points.

To expedite trading, one Dutch ship took two sons of a sachem with them back to Holland, where they might learn the language and religion and become intermediaries. This did not work out so well because one of the young men later killed the captain of the ship. Another Dutch ship dropped off a mulatto man with trade goods to stay and get to know the Indians.

Some of the early Dutch trading voyages also explored other regions along the coast. Adrian Block "discovered" Block Island in 1614, which, of course, was already inhabited by Indians, and his ship, the *Tyger*, accidentally burned to the waterline while moored along Manhattan Island. Over the winter, he and his men (with some help from the Lenni-Lenape) put together another ship which they sailed through Long Island Sound, taking him by the island. Block then explored and laid Dutch claim to the Housatonic River, the Connecticut River (which the Dutch referred to as "the Fresh River") and Narragansett Bay. Block's map was the first to use the term, "New Netherland."

Block

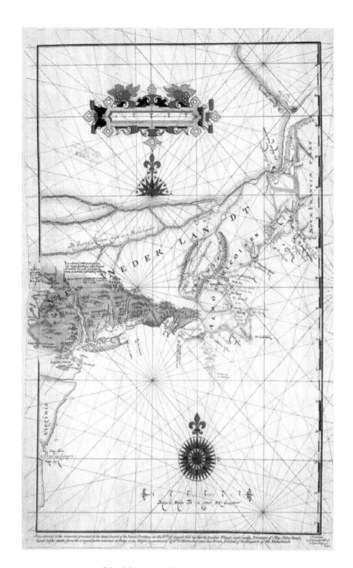

Block's map of New Netherland

Jim Henderson's picture of a replica of Block's boat docked in Manhattan

During this early time period, other Dutch ships sailed south and laid claim to the Delaware River area (which had been briefly visited by Hudson). Cornelius May (for whom Cape May is named) in 1613 and Cornelius Hendricksen in 1614 explored that region and mapped it. During the Dutch period, the Delaware River was called the "South River," with the Hudson being the "North River." Until the take-over of New Netherland by the English in 1664, and with the exception of a few years when there was a New Sweden on the lower Delaware River (founded in 1638 and destroyed by the Dutch in 1655), this whole long stretch of the coastal territories from the bottom of Cape Cod on the north to the Delaware River and Bay on the south was under the control of the Dutch, with the English to the north and south of them.

The Hudson River Valley and the river's mouth was the Dutch heartland. Pursuing the fur trade with the Indians, Capt. Hendrick Corstiaensen in 1614 established a fortified trading post, Ft. Nassau (named after the House of Orange), on Castle Island in the Hudson River near present-day Albany, where they commenced trade with the local Mahican Indians for furs. That fort was abandoned after flooding in 1617.

Several years later in 1624, the Dutch West India Company, which had been put in control of New Netherland, built Ft. Orange to take advantage of the same confluence of rivers and Indian trails. This fort was located some two miles north of the former Ft. Nassau. In a report from 1628, it's stated that 25 or 26 traders were stationed at the fort, but no families.

Furs brought in by the Indians poured out of the backcountry – and wealth into the coffers of the Dutch merchants. One ship alone, the *Arms of Amsterdam*, carried back home from New Netherland in 1626 a cargo consisting of 7,246 beaver pelts, 853 ½ otter skins, 81 mink skins, 36 wild cat skins, and others, plus samples of grain now being grown. The skins were worth 45,000 guilders. By 1634, a village had grown up around Ft. Orange and had acquired an identity of its own: the aptly-named *Beverwyck*.

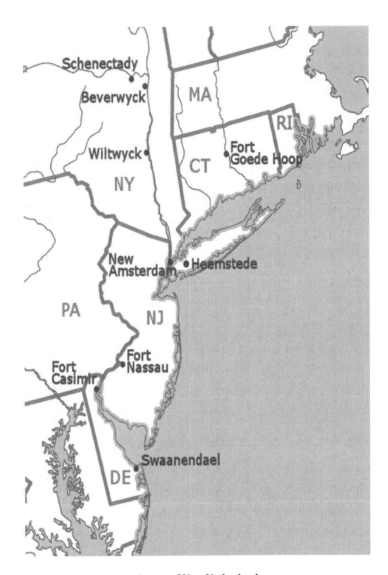

A map of New Netherland

Unlike their fellow Calvinists in the neighboring Pilgrim and Puritan colonies of New England, the Dutch did not come to New Netherland for religious purposes. They came primarily to make money. Many of the early comers were young single men who, while supposed to farm or carry on a craft, were often attracted to make money in the beaver trade.

The first Dutch families arrived at New Amsterdam in 1624 and settled on *Noten Eylant* ("Nut Island"), which the Indians called "Pagganck" (the same meaning) because of its many chestnut, hickory, and oak trees. It's now known as Governor's Island. Some were sent out to Ft. Orange and outlying Dutch settlements on the Delaware River, but they were quickly pulled back for fear that they could not be defended or supported there.

A director appointed by the West India Company was the person on the scene in charge of trade and colonization, and he governed with the help of a council. Under the directorship of Willem Verhulst, construction began in 1625 on Ft. Amsterdam at the lower west bottom of Manhattan across from Governor's Island. Today, the seal of New York City, which depicts a Dutch sailor with his navigation tools, an Indian holding a bow, four windmills blades, two flour barrels and two beavers, marks that year, 1625, as the date of its founding.

New York City's seal

Even so, it was not until the 1626 that Peter Minuit, the West India Company's next director, purchased Manhattan Island from the local Lenni-Lenape for 60 guilders worth of trade goods. This provides the origins of the fable about some of the most expensive real estate in the world being purchased for $24 (although that amount would be worth quite a bit more today). The Indians' concept of property was based on use-rights, not exclusivity, and that is probably what they thought they were agreeing to share. Staten Island (named for the *States General*) was acquired in a similar transaction in 1626, while the other great borough of what became New York City, Brooklyn, was acquired in 1646.

Minuit

Minuit, like many of New Netherland's earliest settlers, was a Walloon – a person hailing from the southern French-speaking provinces of the Netherlands – who had fled Spanish control because he was a Protestant. He was subsequently seeking to rebuild his life somewhere else, so he and others came America. New Amsterdam during Peter Minuit's stint (he served as director until 1632) consisted of 30 log houses around the fort headquarters at the southern tip of Manhattan Island, and under his charge when he took over were approximately 200 people.

In 1625, the West India Company contracted for ships to carry livestock, farm tools, plants and seeds to the new colony, and the next year, Isaack de Rasiere, Minuit's second-in-charge as the colony's secretary, reported to a company director in Amsterdam that there were six Dutch farms now operating on Manhattan. Farm No. One, near the East River, was the farm of the director.

A 1639 map shows more farms and plantations existing by that time on Manhattan north to Morningside Heights and Harlem, across the Hudson in what is now New Jersey, and on Long Island. Tobacco was grown on some of the plantations, and ever since the 17th century, the area of lower Manhattan east of today's Little Italy and north of Chinatown has been known as "the Bowery," deriving its name from the old Dutch word for farms ("bouwerji"). The 1639 map also shows a grist mill and a saw mill existing close by the fort and another saw mill located out on Governor's Island. Ft. Amsterdam was completed in 1635. It consisted of a brick interior with an earth and turf exterior. The shape of the fort, following state-of-the-art European military design, was a quadrangle with a bastion at each of the four corners. Along with protecting the colony from attack, another important task of the authorities was to establish a church. The first communion in a Dutch Reformed Church under Rev. Jonas Michaelius took place in 1628; the first church building was built in 1633.

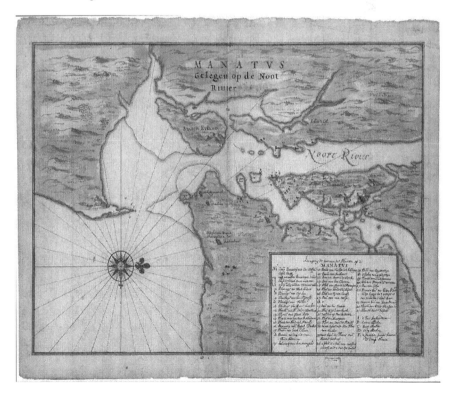

The 1639 map of New Amsterdam

Early on, the West India Company also set up two small fortified trading posts (*factorij*) on the "South River" (Delaware River). One was on Verhulsten Island (Burlington Island today) in the Delaware River near present-day Trenton, New Jersey. Ft. Wilhelmus (named for a popular song about the Dutch hero William of Orange) was built there in 1625. However, in 1626, these settlers were recalled to focus colonization efforts in the Hudson River Valley.

Fort Nassau, erected farther down the Delaware River near present-day Gloucester City, N.J. across the river from present-day Philadelphia, became a more permanent outpost lasting until the 1650s. From that location, trade in furs was conducted with the Lenni-Lenape and the Susquehannocks, a Iroquoian-speaking people who lived on the river by that name. The Susquehannocks had sent a delegation to New Amsterdam soliciting a closer Dutch presence.

On the "Fresh River" (Connecticut River), the Dutch paid the dominant local Pequot Indians for permission to establish a fortified trading post, the *Huys de Hoop* (House of Hope) south of present-day Hartford in 1633. This was intended to hold down the colony's north border, but problems soon arose in that vicinity because the English set up their own rival trade post.

To attract more settlers to New Netherland, the West India Company instituted a new policy in 1629 whereby wealthy individuals and groups of individuals could be granted large pieces of the colony's territory and essentially become feudal lords – *patroons* – with almost total authority over that territory and its inhabitants. In order to become a *patroon*, what one needed to do was to agree to bring 50 adults to an area of the colony that was not Manhattan within a period of four years. Their fiefdom could extend 16 miles along a navigable river or eight miles on both sides and an unlimited distance into the backcountry. Settlers would be rent-paying tenants who could not leave without the permission of the *patron*, and *patroons* held a monopoly on hunting, fishing and milling grain.

On these terms, *patroonages* were established along the Hudson and Delaware Rivers, but the only *patroonage* that lasted and proved successful was the one located on the upper reaches of the Hudson near present-day Albany. This was *Rensselaerswyck*, which was granted to one of the Company's directors, the wealthy Amsterdam jewel merchant Kiliaen van Rensselaer. Land was purchased from the Indians, and colonists, along with livestock and farming tools, were dispatched from the Netherlands, arriving in June 1630. Rensselaer's original plan was for his tenants to raise wheat and other provisions to exchange for sugar produced by the Dutch slave plantations in Brazil. However, in its early years, *Rensselaerswyck* was successful not so much from any agricultural pursuits but due to its proximity to Ft. Orange and accessibility to the fur trade.

Kiliaen van Rensselaer

A small colony called *Swanendael* established by several *patroons* in 1631 on the south side of Delaware Bay to hunt whales and to grow grain and tobacco for export to the Netherlands came to a tragic end. The settlers had erected a piece of tin showing the arms of Holland on a column, and not knowing any better, a local Lenni-Lenape sachem had taken it to make tobacco pipes. Some Indians who thought they were helping the Dutch then killed the sachem, but that set in motion a cycle of revenge in which other Indians wiped out all 32 of the settlers. After that bad reversal, the Dutch did not return immediately to the Lower Delaware region. That left a vacancy into which Swedes and Finns moved in 1638 and founded New Sweden.

The first regulations that the West India Company had issued in 1624 for the colonists in New

Netherland specified, among other things, that "they shall take especial care, whether in trading or in other matters" to stay on good terms with and to fulfill promises made to the Indians. They could also carry on inland trade provided that they sold exclusively to the Company. As all of this indicates, the Dutch colonists generally did not seize land from the native inhabitants, and although it's fair to question the dealings, the Dutch typically signed deeds of sale with the natives in the European manner.

To trade with the Indians, the Dutch imported kettles, axes, hatchets and a considerable amount of duffle (a course woolen cloth). Since the item most desired by the Indians was *wampum*, the Dutch acquired it from the tribes who manufactured it along Long Island Sound and exchanged it for furs with Indians in the interior. They even began to trade with black and white beads of their own manufacture, although the Indians were quite able to distinguish the genuine article from the knock-offs.

Chapter 5: War

The Dutch tried to maintain good relations with all of the tribes for the sake of healthy trade but found themselves in the middle of conflicts among some of them, conflicts exacerbated by the fur trade. At Ft. Orange on the upper Hudson River, the powerful Mohawks of the Iroquois Confederacy challenged the Mahicans for access to the Dutch traders and attempted to become the middlemen with more inland tribes, so the Mahicans were forced to cede their land and relocate to the eastern side of the river.

In time, Indians who lived closer to New Amsterdam felt uncomfortable because the Dutch at Ft. Orange had traded guns to their Mohawk enemies while they still had none to defend themselves. An additional factor causing Indians discomfort was the depletion of the fur-bearing animals with which they could trade for the commodities upon which they had become dependent.

As Dutch populations grew and expanded, the Indians became increasingly upset. By 1640, the Dutch had spread out from Manhattan and established new settlements on Staten Island, Long Island, and in the Bronx, which was named for Jonas Bronck after he settled there in 1639. They also settled in what is now Westchester County and New Jersey.

In September 1639, the relatively new director of the colony, Willem Kieft, set in motion a chain of events that led to warfare between the Dutch and some of the Lenni-Lenape around New Amsterdam when he demanded the Indians pay a tribute consisting of wampum, furs and corn. The 19th century historian, John Romeyn Brodhead, observed that this move on Kieft's part, which made sense from his point of view as a tax for services rendered by the Dutch to the Indians , understandably caused very strong ill feelings among the Indians. "They wondered how the sachem at the fort dared to exact such things from them.' 'He must be a very shabby fellow; he had come to live in their land when they had not invited him, and now came to deprive them of their corn for nothing.' They refused to pay the contribution, because the soldiers in Fort Amsterdam were no protection to the savages, who should not be called upon for their support; because they had allowed the Dutch to live peaceably in their country, and had never demanded recompense; because when the Hollanders, 'having lost a ship there, had built a new one, they had supplied them with victuals and all other necessaries, and had taken care of them for two winters, until the ship was finished,' and therefore the Dutch were under obligations to them; because they had paid full price for every thing they had purchased, and there was, therefore, no reason why they should supply the Hollanders now 'with maize for nothing;' and, finally, said the savages, because, 'if we have ceded to you the country you are living in, we yet remain masters of what we have retained for ourselves.'"

Kieft

Ultimately, warfare broke out in 1640. The Raritan band of the Lenni-Lenape were blamed for killing some pigs belonging to white settlers on Staten Island – white settlers typically let their swine run at large to forage in the woods -- although other evidence points to some servants of the Company as being the real culprits. Kieft decided that this was the right moment to show the Indians who was boss; he sent his secretary with a party of soldiers and sailors to demand reparations from the Indians and, if that were not forthcoming, to take as many of them as possible prisoner and destroy their corn fields. As a result, Dutch soldiers killed several Indians and took prisoner the brother of the sachem, and one of the soldiers on the boat back to Manhattan used a split piece of wood to torture the genitalia of the captured Indian.

Although the sachem's brother was released after the payment of a wampum ransom, the Indians remained determined to take revenge against the Dutch for equating their lives with the lives of swine. This came about the following year in June 1641 when the Raritans attacked the farm of David de Vries on Staten Island and killed four of his servants in the process of burning the farm and another nearby one. Kieft now offered a wampum reward to other Indians to bring in the culprits, dead or alive, and to preserve the peace with the Dutch, some other Lenni-Lenape killed some of the Raritans.

This put an end to the warfare between the Raritans and the Dutch, but in August 1641, an incident involving another Lenni-Lenape band, the Wecquaesgeeks (who lived north of Manhattan in what is now the Bronx and Westchester County), led to more warfare. After a Wecquaesgeek man killed a Dutch trader who lived there and plundered his house, Kieft demanded that the murderer be turned over to the Dutch for justice, but the Wecquaesgeek sachem refused, arguing the man was getting revenge for a murder of a relative committed by Dutch servants 21 years before. This may have made cultural sense to the Indians but not to the Dutch governor, and after much debate about whether starting an Indian war was the right thing for the colony – De Vries argued for leniency -- an expedition was sent out from New Amsterdam in March 1642 to attack the Wecquaesgeek village.

The expedition got lost and never found the village, but the intimidated Wecquaesgeeks asked the Dutch for peace and believed that they had obtained it. Later in 1642, a Dutchman was killed by a member of the Hackensack band of Lenni-Lenape while under the influence of alcohol, and after that, Kieft was convinced that there was some kind of general Indian conspiracy afoot to wipe out the whites. Kieft refused to accept the wampum offered by the Wecquaesgeek sachems -- the traditional Indian way of handling such matters -- and demanded that the murderer be turned over for Dutch justice. The sachems blamed alcohol for the incident and asked for its distribution to the Indians to be curtailed. As ethnohistorian Evan Haefeli has observed in his brilliant treatment of the cultural misunderstandings that led to Kieft's Lenni-Lenape War, "Kieft's demands that the sachems turn over one of their own people to Dutch justice could never be met. Unlike Kieft, the sachems did not have coercive power over their people. Turning a member of their village over to certain death would have brought the vengeance of the killer's family on the sachems' heads. It would be akin to betraying them to the enemy. By refusing to accept gifts as atonement for the killings, or to even offer gifts in exchange for the man they requested, Kieft was acting as any enemy. The sachems were in a truly awkward position.

Unable to get Kieft to stop behaving as an enemy but unwilling to stop being allies of the Dutch, the sachems laughed, hoping the conflicting demands could be shrugged off before they became dangerous. Perhaps, like children, the Dutch would realize that they were doing the wrong thing."

For his part, Kieft thought he was being disrespected by the Indians, something he felt that a man in his position could not tolerate any longer. Thus, when the Wecquaesgeeks (who thought the Dutch were their friends again) came to the Dutch seeking protection from the Mahicans, who had been attacking them, Kieft did the opposite and instead ordered soldiers to make a night assault on the two unsuspecting refugee camps near New Amsterdam. 120 Indians were brutally killed and mutilated, an outcome that was equally horrifying to many of the Dutch.

A new war of revenge now spread to Long Island as the Indians burned farms and ambushed settlers. The fighting ended temporarily in the spring of 1643, when the Canarsee band of Lenni-Lenape on Long Island and the Hackensacks made their peace with the Dutch in order to get on with corn planting, but even so, the Indians felt the presents they received from Kieft at the peace talks were insufficient compensation for the loss of lives. Young warriors in particular wanted to exact more revenge on the whites, as the sachems informed the Kieft, suggesting that more presents needed to be forthcoming from the Dutch to satisfy their anger. Governor Kieft, locked in his culture's way of thinking about power, could not understand why the sachems simply did not have the disobedient warriors killed, much the same way he had recently ordered a servant who tried to assassinate him executed.

Thus, war broke out again in August 1643, this time including previously uninvolved Indians: the Wappingers, who were closely related to the Lenni-Lenape and lived along the eastern side of the Hudson River. The initial violent act came when Wappingers attacked a boat laden with beaver furs coming down the river from Ft. Orange and made off with the furs after killing two of the crewmen. Other Indians attacked other boats on the river, resulting in deaths on both sides. In September, the Indians on Long Island attacked farms and killed settlers there, after which terrified colonists fled to New Amsterdam or took ship back to Europe. It was during this time that a wall was built across lower Manhattan, and it ended up lending its name to Wall Street.

Unable to cope with the badly deteriorating situation on their own, the Dutch authorities hired English soldiers under Capt. John Underhill to supplement their own. Underhill had been one of the leaders in New England's recent war against the Pequots, which had broken that tribe's power. In October, after the harvest season, Underhill attacked Indian villages on Long Island and killed any Indians they could find. Most fled, but the whites also destroyed their corn crops.

In 1637, during the Pequot War, Underhill's men had surrounded and burned an Indian fort near present-day Mystic, Connecticut, killing 400 Pequots, including women and children. A similar massacre took place in February 1644 when Underhill surrounded and set fire to an

Indian encampment, mercilessly killing over 500 Wappingers and other Indians present.

This European version of total war was not the Indian way of war, and they were devastated, so in March 1644, the Wecquaesgeeks and Wappingers made peace with the Dutch. In August 1645 a general peace treaty was signed at New Amsterdam by Kieft and his council, with some Lenni-Lenape sachems agreeing that further conflicts would be settled not through violence but through complaints taken to the sachems and the Dutch authorities. To reduce chances for violence, the treaty specified that Indians would not come into New Amsterdam, nor would the Dutch come into the Indian villages with their guns.

This peace treaty with the Lenni-Lenape held fast, but ultimately, Kieft was removed from his position as colony director, and on his way back home to Amsterdam to try to justify his conduct, his ship was lost at sea. The new director replacing Kieft was Peter Stuyvesant, with whom New Netherland would be associated for the rest of its existence until it was taken over by the English in 1664. Under his tenure, there would be two further wars between other Indian tribes and the Dutch: the "Peach War" with the Susquehannocks in 1655 and a long war with the Esopus from 1659-1663.

Stuyvesant

Things were not much more civilized in New Amsterdam when Stuyvesant took over in 1647. The residents, to him, had "grown wild and were loose in their morals." With his peg leg in tow (part of Stuyvesant's right leg had been amputated due to a cannonball hit during his stint in the Caribbean), the staunch Calvinist began to make some serious changes. No longer could livestock roam free with abandon, or garbage be thrown into the streets, which were now to be paved in cobblestones (the first such street was the now aptly named Stone Street). Dangerous wooden chimneys and other combustible building materials were outlawed, and a sort of fire department was established. However, alms for the poor, orphanages, and schools received less or grudging support—as they continue to do today. Many decrees were issued; in fact, the first law against driving too fast was passed in 1657. Stuyvesant's "civilizing" mission helped a new, more regulated and stratified society form, one with a newly wealthy merchant class and, of course, many classes below them.

In 1639, the West India Company relaxed its monopoly on trade with New Netherland. To stimulate the colony's economy and to attract more settlers, the doors were opened wide for merchants throughout the United Provinces and merchants from all other friendly nations to trade, as long as they paid certain import and export duties to the Company. Until 1651, when England imposed the Navigation Act, the merchants of New Netherland could also trade profitably with New England and Virginia.

The population grew, but even still, the non-Indian population of New Netherland was just 3,500 in 1655 and grew to no more than 9,000 or so by 1664. The English colonies to the North and South grew much faster during the same time period; for example, Massachusetts Bay had 20,000 colonists in 1660 and Virginia had over 27,000.

Adriaen Van der Donck was New Netherland's first lawyer. He took ship from Amsterdam to *Rensselaerswyck* in 1642 and subsequently purchased land from the Indians for an estate at Yonkers, just north of Manhattan and the Bronx. In fact, the name Yonkers was derived from his name. Van der Donck wrote *A Description of the New Netherlands (As the Same are at the Present Time)* that was published in Amsterdam in 1653, and the principle intent of this tract was apparently to encourage greater settlement. As such, it described natural resources such as the "multitudes of beavers" and the numerous whales to be hunted profitably, the salubrious streams and spring waters, fertile soils, fine woods for ships, house-building and fire wood, valuable minerals, and more. However, the problem for the colony was that quick profits available from the fur trade would never be overcome by any other resources.

Van der Donck

Despite having less people, New Netherland (and especially New Amsterdam) was already in much more diverse than any of the English-speaking colonies. According to a Jesuit priest who passed through in 1643, New Amsterdam had speakers of no fewer than 18 different languages, and half of the population of New Netherland may have been non-Dutch. Along with the previously mentioned Walloons, many residents were Germans and French Huguenots, and a fair number were Scandinavians. Around the mid-17th century, the first Jews arrived in New Amsterdam from Brazil, becoming the earliest Jews in any of the colonies that would go on to become states in the United States. The 1639 map shows an encampment on Manhattan for black slaves, and, after mid-century, the numbers of slaves greatly increased as ships brought more to the colony directly from Africa. New York would subsequently have the largest urban population of African-Americans in the northern English colonies.

A depiction of slaves being sold in New Amsterdam in 1655

In its diverse makeup, New Amsterdam had resembled Old Amsterdam, which was a city renowned for its tolerance of different religions, but Stuyvesant's hard-nosed Calvinism made him intolerant of other religions; he attempted to outlaw all but his own, and to expel Jews who arrived in the 1650s. The West India Company, however, forced him to reverse his decree: the Company was interested in harvesting the wealth and services such new immigrants could provide. Of course, the slaves who were owned by the Company had much bleaker prospects in New Amsterdam, including those who could eventually be set free under the Company's policies (slaves were often set free when they were too old or lame to be "useful," and could not otherwise earn their own keep easily in such a society). Moreover, under Stuyvesant, New

Amsterdam became a major port in the slave trade.

Stuyvesant sought to set prices in all kinds of markets to eliminate fraud and issued licenses and held inspections, but many purveyors and artisans balked at these controls. From the very beginning of what would become the financial capital of the world, inflation and double-dealing were evident. The Dutch treated wampum—strings of beads made from shells that the Lenapes used as currency—as legal tender. Wampum was often considered more valuable to Native Americans than European goods, and bartering gave way to the abstract value of "money." (Alcohol, too, was often given to Native Americans to lubricate deals.) Very soon, wampum knock-offs, made of inferior beads and other illegitimate elements, began circulating. By the time of Stuyvesant's reign as Director-General, inconsistencies in wampum were out of control, forcing him to regulate its manufacture and value.

In 1652, England and the Netherlands were at war, but heavy losses on both sides hurried the prospect of peace. Nevertheless, the two countries' representatives in the New World were increasingly hostile toward each other, even though they were an ocean away from the main belligerents. The Puritans of New England were said to be intent on attacking Manhattan, so preparations were made in New Amsterdam. A wall would be erected at New Amsterdam's northern border, at a cost of 5,000 guilders, with the labor being cheaply supplied by slaves. Made of 15 foot planks, bastions, cannons, and two gates (one at the corner of present-day Wall and Pearl, the other at Wall and Broadway) the location of the wall would become not a barrier to invasion but the center of the financial world.

In the meantime, however, the wall ultimately proved as useless as all other Dutch defenses and strategies. In 1664, Colonel Richard Niccolls was sent by the English Duke of York to take Manhattan and all other Dutch holdings. Niccolls sent Stuyvesant a letter that promised life and liberty for all if the inhabitants would lay down their arms and surrender. Stuyvesant hid this letter and tore up another, but powerful residents in New Amsterdam forced him to give up in the face of too formidable an enemy. In the end, the diversity of New Amsterdam helped assure that the people would rather become part of New York City than lose everything. The Dutch briefly reclaimed the city, but the tide had turned, and New York became an English settlement. For their own part, the Lenni-Lenape who had lived there for so long dwindled until there were only about 200 of them left at the beginning of the 18th century.

A map of New Amsterdam in 1660

Jean Leon Gerome Ferris' "The Fall of New Amsterdam"

New Amsterdam lasted for less than 50 years, but with Dutch names and Indian names sprinkled across the landscape, it clearly left a considerable legacy to the future New York City as a commercial center and as a major cultural and ethnic melting pot. Russell Shorto was totally on the mark in his recent book on Manhattan, *The Island at the Center of the World*, when he concluded that the Dutch colony, with its sense of free trade, tolerance and multiculturalism, was the forerunner of the modern United States.

Online Resources

Other books about New York City by Charles River Editors

The Lost Colony of Roanoke and Jamestown: The History and Legacy of England's First American Colonies by Charles River Editors

American Legends: The Pilgrims and the Mayflower by Charles River Editors

Bibliography

Asher, Georg Michael, ed. *Henry Hudson the Navigator: The Original Documents in Which*

His Career Is Recorded. London: Hakluyt Society, 1860.

Braudel, Fernand. *Civilization and Capitalism, 15th-18th Century: The Perspective of the World.* University of California Press, 1982.

Brodhead, John Romeyn. *History of the State of New York.* Vol. 1. New York: Harper & Brothers, 1853.

Cohen, David Steven. "How Dutch Were the Dutch of New Netherland?" *New York History,* 1981, 43–60.

Compagnie, Nederlandsche West-Indische. *Documents Relating to New Netherland 1624-1626 in the Henry E. Huntington Library.* Henry E. Huntington Library and Art Gallery, 1924.

Danckaerts, Jasper, and Peter Sluyter. *Journal of a Voyage to New York and a Tour in Several of the American Colonies in 1679-80.* Vol. 1. *Memoirs of the Long Island Historical Society.* Brooklyn, N.Y.: Gregg Press, 1867.

Goddard, Ives. "The Origin and Meaning of the Name' Manhattan.'" *New York History,* 2010, 277–93.

Haefeli, Evan. "Kieft's War and the Cultures of Violence in Colonial America." In *Lethal Imagination: Violence and Brutality in American History,* edited by Michael A. Bellesiles, 17–40. New York: NYU Press, 1999.

Holm, Thomas Campanius, ed. *Description of the Province of New Sweden: Now Called, by the English, Pennsylvania, in America.* Philadelphia, 1834.

Howell, George Rogers, and Jonathan Tenney. *Bi-Centennial History of Albany: History of the County of Albany, N. Y., from 1609 to 1886.* Vol. 4. New York: W. W. Munsell & Company, 1886.

Jameson, J. Franklin, ed. *Narratives of New Netherland, 1609-1664*. New York: Charles Scribner's Sons, 1909.

Myers, Albert Cook, ed. *Narratives of Early Pennsylvania, West New Jersey and Delaware, 1630-1707. Original Narratives of Early American History*. New York: Charles Scribner's Sons, 1912.

New York Historical Society. *Collections of the New-York Historical Society*, 2nd Ser., 1 (1841).

Penn, William. *William Penn's Own Account of the Lenni Lenape Or Delaware Indians*. Hurst, Texas: B & A Publishers, 1981.

Rink, Oliver A. *Holland on the Hudson: An Economic and Social History of Dutch New York*. Reprint edition. Ithaca, N.Y.: Cornell University Press, 1989.

Shaw, William, ed. History of Essex and Hudson Counties, New Jersey. Vol. 2. Philadelphia: Everts & Peck, 1884.

Shorto, Russell. *The Island at the Center of the World*. New York: Knopf Doubleday Publishing Group, 2005.

Trigger, Bruce G., ed. *Handbook of North American Indians*. Vol. 15. *Northeast*. Washington D.C.: Smithsonian Institution, 1978.

Vries, Jan de. *The First Modern Economy: Success, Failure, and Perseverance of the Dutch Economy, 1500-1815*. Cambridge: Cambridge University Press, 1997.

Weslager, Professor C. A. *The Delaware Indians: A History*. Reprint edition. New Brunswick, N.J.: Rutgers University Press, 1990.

Winkle, Edward Van. *Manhattan, 1624-1639*. New York: Knickerbocker Press, 1916.

Wolley, Charles. *A Two Years' Journal in New York and Part of Its Territories in America*. Cleveland: The Burrows Brothers Company, 1902.

Made in the USA
Middletown, DE
13 January 2021